Meditation
John of the Cross

Meditations With

John of the Cross

versions by
Camille Anne Campbell

BEAR & COMPANY
SANTA FE, NEW MEXICO

Library of Congress Cataloging-in-Publication Data
John of the Cross, Saint, 1542-1591.
    Meditations with John of the Cross / preface and versions by
Camille Anne Campbell; introduction by Ernest E. Larkin.
        p.   cm.
    ISBN 0-939680-62-9
    1. Spiritual life—Catholic authors—Early works to 1800. 2. Medita-
tions—Early works to 1800.   I. Campbell, Camille Anne. II. Title.
BX2179.J63   1989
242—dc19   88-32911
                                                              CIP

Bear & Company
P.O. Drawer 2860
Santa Fe, NM 87504

Design & illustrations: Kathleen Katz
Typography: Buffalo Publications
Printed in the United States of American by Banta

9 8 7 6 5 4 3 2

Contents

Introduction

The Carmelite martyr of Dachau, Blessed Titus Brandsma, remarked that John of the Cross is a Marian theologian, because his entire teaching is about Christ being formed in us. His topic is Christogenesis, the full revelation of the sons and daughters of God (Rom 8:19).

John presents the process after the beginnings have been consolidated. He comes to the rescue of souls searching for the fullness of the divine presence and floundering for lack of direction. He zeroes into the heart of the matter and reduces the journey to the twin tasks of letting go of the world and letting God take hold.

The single goal is to let Christ be formed in you (Gal 4:19). Fix your eyes on Jesus, ne says, so that his image is engraved in your being, your consciousness transformed, and your life configured to that of the Son of God, the Wisdom of God. This new birthing in Christ Jesus is the core of Christianity, and John describes its fullness this side of heaven. It is divine union, the fullest appropriation of the paschal mystery of dying and rising with Christ.

John picks up the journey in a period of involution, when the old ways of positively relating to God through the gifts of creation are losing their effectiveness and appeal. The limitations, the disappointments and betrayals, the mortality of all things human as bridges to the divine are beginning to be felt like stone walls of impasse. The woundedness of life is showing up. The soul perceives itself as regressing and easily falls into self-doubt. But what looks like bad news, John tells us, is actually good news. These negative experiences are the womb of the divine. They reveal the God who is always beyond his creation. He comes through the cracks and limits of human experiences.

In traditional terms the search for divine union is entering the phase of contemplation. The bits-and-pieces approach of discursive activity is giving way to the deeper and more real presence of Christ within. Efforts to organize and integrate one's outer world give way to the inner work of transformation in one's loves and desires. There is disorientation and darkness in this period of incubation — it is the famous "dark night" of John of the Cross — but a new configuration of relationships with the world is in formation.

Does this development take the disciple of John of the Cross outside the perspectives of creation-centered spirituality? Assuredly not. Think only of John's poetry which is brimming with joy in God's creation. John is no world-hater or anti-creationist; he is solidly in the great Catholic company of Christian humanists. If anything, he is antagonist only against those who love the world too little.

His way of detachment is the only way to God, but paradoxically it is the only way to loving the world in its truth and fullness. This benefit, he remarks wryly, is justification enough for the rugged asceticism he proposes. Love God, he says, and the world will come alive. Love the world without God and you are loving a feeble reflection of your own self. The two gifts of God and his creation are intertwined and inseparable. The mystic cries out ecstatically:

> My Beloved *is* the mountains
> And lonely wooded valleys . . .

All this is the very positive doctrine that Sister Camille Ann Campbell offers in capsule form in this beautiful little book of *Meditations with John of the Cross.* She chooses themes from each of the four major prose works to nourish reflection on the central task of putting on the Lord Jesus Christ. Morsels of mystical teaching are offered for reflection, and her hope is to bring the reader to the full menu of the poetry and extended prose commentaries of John himself.

The poetry particularly can complement these selections and be read along simultaneously. The poems represent the first and most direct attempt to seize in words the inexpressible experience of the soul with God. They are art objects, symbols that contain and evoke the experience in a real way. In a sense all the rest, the prose, is talk. Talk can help, but even in John's own mind the commentaries are secondary and never supplant the poems.

These pages, selected and authored by Sister Camille Ann, are simplifications of the theologizing of St. John of the Cross on the soul's transformation. They are excellent introductions in the style of the author's earlier *Meditations with Teresa of Avila.* May all the volumes in this series lead contemporary searchers for union with God to the source of all wisdom who is Christ himself. And may Sister Camille Ann be blessed in her gifted ministry of enlisting the Carmelite mystics in this work.

Ernest E. Larkin, O.Carm.
Kino Institute
Phoenix, Arizona

Preface and Acknowledgements

John of the Cross wrote of the soul's journey in this life to union with God in love, culminating in the spiritual marriage of the soul with God. His writings are detailed, complete, deep, sublime and, most of all, challenging. In an age when greed seems to reign, accumulating goods seems to be the goal of many, and satisfaction of all one's desires an endless pursuit, one might wonder why anyone would read a work by him or about his work.

It is also an age of deprivation, of injustice, of grossly uneven distribution of wealth, of dead ends in trying to satisfy all desires, even to dependency on chemical substances. It is an age when many are satiated but empty.

The truly poor and empty are hungry for a message which brings them hope which reveals to them that part of the life process is letting go of things, letting go of the desire for more and more. It is letting be the gifts of life the Creator has given to them, and always asking for the supreme gift of love. John of the Cross has a message of hope.

John of the Cross writes for those who have gone beyond the stage of beginners, and who sincerely desire to be more closely united to God. He tells us how we can open our minds and hearts to the letting go and letting be which must necessarily and ultimately occur at the end of our journey through this life. He challenges us to be actively involved in the transformation of our souls and of our world.

The many powerful and beautiful references to creation reveal how creation-centered John of the Cross was. The many analogies drawn from nature reveal deep truths about our journey to union with God. From knowing God through creatures, John explains in detail the wonderful, joyful, delightful experience of knowing creatures through God.

These meditations are taken from John's commentaries on the poetry written by him to help his readers comprehend the deep meaning contained in the verses. To fully appreciate the meditations it is important to also read the verses. I hope the reader will be inspired to read the complete works of St. John of the Cross.

Each section of this work is based upon one of the major works of John of the Cross. The first section is drawn from *The Ascent of Mount Carmel*; the second from *The Dark Night of the Soul*; the third and fourth are based on *The Spiritual Canticle* and *The Living Flame of Love*, respectively. It is my hope that this will serve as a guide for the reader and that it will lead one to the original works.

My work on *Meditations with John of the Cross* filled me with awe for the depth and realism of his work. It was truly a challenge to examine my own life and my own struggle for the union with God in love.

I chose quotations from the translations of *The Collected Works of St. John of the Cross*, copyright 1973, ICS Publications, Washington, D.C. A special thanks to the Institute of Carmelite Studies for their permission to use the work.

I thank those who have encouraged me to do the book and who have helped me in my own journey. Matthew Fox, O.P., director of the Institute of Culture and Creation Spirituality and my thesis advisor on creation-centered spirituality in Teresa of Avila and John of the Cross, first challenged me to do the Meditations books on Teresa and then on John of the Cross. My family has always encouraged me to use any talents I have, especially my

English-teacher mother who edited the final manuscript. My friend Beth Ann Simno diligently typed and retyped the manuscript. Finally, I thank the Carmelite sisters of my community, especially Sister Mary Edward Romagosa, Ph.D. who corrected the manuscript for me.

Last of all, I thank you who have chosen to read the work. May it be of some benefit to you in your own journey to the Lord.

Preparing For The Journey

*Not to let go
is like planting a seed
in untilled soil*

The Journey

Do you wish to advance from the stage of a beginner in your journey to union with God? Do you desire to love enough to reach the divine light of perfect union with God? God gives many souls the talent and grace for advancing.

It is sad to see people continue in a beginner's method of communion with God because they do not want or know how to advance, or because they receive no direction for breaking away from the methods of beginners. They resemble children who kick, cry and struggle to walk by themselves when their mothers want to carry them. In walking by themselves they make no headway, or if they do, it is at a child's pace.

What Is
The Journey Like?

The soul must ordinarily pass through two principal kinds of night in order to reach union with God. The first night concerns the sensory part of one's soul; the second, the spiritual part.

This letting go is called a night because the soul journeys in darkness as though by night.

The first night is the lot of beginners at the time God commences to introduce them to a state of contemplation.

The second night takes place in those who are already experienced at the time God desires to lead them to divine union.

The Dark Night

This journey is a dark night because the individual must not cling to any worldly possessions. This is a night for the senses because the road one travels is faith. And for the intellect this is like a dark night because the point of arrival is God, a dark night to us in this life.

In speaking of these nights of letting go and letting be we are not discussing the mere lack of things. This lack will not free the soul if it craves all these objects and desires to cling to them.

The things of the world are not themselves an encumbrance or harm to the soul; rather it is the will and appetite dwelling within it which cause the damage.

Darkness, which is a clinging to creatures, and light, which is God, are contraries. All the creatures of heaven and earth are nothing when compared to God.

It is ignorant to think one can reach this union with God without first emptying the appetite of all natural and supernatural things that can be a hindrance.

What is given in this union is transformation in God. "One who does not renounce all possessions with his will cannot be my disciple." (Lk 14:33)

Creatures are crumbs that fall from the Master's table. One who clings to things is always dissatisfied and bitter like someone who is hungry.

God accomplishes more in cleansing and purging a person than He does in creating the person from nothing because there is no opposition in creation.

Clinging

Clinging is like a fire which blazes up when one throws wood on it. The fire dwindles but intensity of appetite does not diminish.

Clinging to things will make the mind dark, the will weak, and the memory dull and disordered. The intellect becomes like murky air in relation to sunlight and cannot receive God's light.

The will becomes incapable of God's embrace of love, like a cloudy mirror. The memory has less capacity for receiving the impression of the serenity of God's image because muddy water cannot reflect one's image clearly.

Thinking this brings union with God, some burden self with penance and other exercises. But these are insufficient if one doesn't diligently strive to let go. Not to let go is like planting a seed in untilled soil or trying to see with a cataract in the eye.

In clinging to things and accomplishments one becomes unhappy with self, cold toward neighbors, sluggish and slothful in the things of God.

It makes no difference whether a bird is tied by a thin thread or a cord. Still it cannot fly.

Not to go forward is to turn back, not to gain ground is to lose. Scripture says: "He that fails in little things will fail in that which is great." (Eccl 19:1) "A great fire is occasioned by a tiny spark." (Eccl 11:34)

A log of wood cannot be transformed into the fire if even a single degree of heat is lacking in its preparation for this.

One can enter the night of sense in two ways: active and passive.

The active way is what one can do and does by oneself to enter the night. In the passive way the individual does nothing, for God accomplishes the work while one acts as a recipient.

A more intense enkindling of another, better love is necessary for the vanquishing of the appetites.

By finding satisfaction and strength in love, one will have the courage and constancy to deny readily all other appetites.

The love of one's spouse is not the only requisite; an enkindling with longings of love is also necessary. How sweet, easy, and delightful the longings make all trials and dangers of this night seem.

Faith, Light
In The Night

The first hours of the night resemble twilight when sensible objects begin to fade from sight. The second part of the night is darker and more interior because it deprives one of rational light, or better, blinds one as at midnight. The final stage of the night before dawn approximates the light of day. God supernaturally illumines the soul with a ray of His divine light.

The first stage, twilight, is darkness to the senses. The second stage, faith, like midnight, is darkness to the spirit. In the third, like the very early dawn just before the light of day, the excessive light of faith is darkness because a brighter light will suppress a dimmer light.

Faith is not a knowledge which comes through the senses, but an ascent of the soul to that which enters through the senses. Faith is a dark night for a person, but in this way gives light. The more darkness it brings, the more light it sheds.

Faith lies beyond all understanding, taste, feeling and imagining that one has. However impressive may be one's knowledge or feeling of God, that knowledge or feeling will have no resemblance to God and amounts to very little.

To attain union with God, a person should advance neither by understanding, nor by the support of one's own experience, nor by feeling or imagination, but by belief in God's being. God's being cannot be grasped by the intellect, appetite, imagination or any other sense, nor can it be known in this life.

Clinging to any understanding, feeling, imagining, desire, opinion, or way of one's own, or to any other work or affairs hinders one from union with God. One must pass beyond everything to unknowing.

In regard to this road to union, entering on the road means leaving one's own road, or better, moving on to the goal; and turning from one's own mode implies entry into what has no mode, that is, God. A person who reaches this state no longer has any methods, nor clings to any methods of understanding, taste, or feeling. Within the self, one possesses all methods, like one who having nothing, possesses all things. (2 Cor 6:10)

An Analogy

A ray of sunlight shining upon a smudgy window is unable to illumine that window completely and transform it into its own light. It could do this if the window were cleaned and polished. The less film and stain are wiped away, the less the window will be illumined. The cleaner the window is, the brighter will be its illumination. The extent of illumination is not dependent upon the ray of sunlight but upon the window. If the window is totally clean and pure, the sunlight will so transform and illumine it that to all appearances the window will be identical with the ray of sunlight and shine just as the sun's ray.

Although obviously the nature of the window is distinct from that of the sun's ray (even if the two seem identical), we can assert that the window is the ray of light of the sun by participation.

The soul, upon which the Divine light of God's being is ever shining and in which it is dwelling by nature, is like this window.

One makes room for God by wiping away all the smudges and smears which come from clinging to creatures, and by uniting the will perfectly to God's, for to love is to labor to divest oneself for God, to let go of all that is not God.

When this is done, the soul will be illumined and transformed in God. And God will so communicate supernatural being to the soul that it will appear to be God and will possess all that God has. God and the soul become one in participant transformation.

Yet its transformed being naturally is distinct from God's just as the window, although illumined by the ray, has an existence distinct from the ray.

Faith, Hope,
Love

The soul is united with God in this life neither through understanding, nor through enjoyment, nor through imagination, nor through any other sense. Only faith, hope, and charity can unite the soul with God in this life.

Faith affirms what cannot be understood by the intellect.

Hope also undoubtedly puts the memory in darkness and emptiness as regards all earthly and heavenly objects. Hope always pertains to the unpossessed object. If something is possessed, there can no longer be hope for it.

Charity, too, causes a void in the will regarding all things, since it obliges us to love God above everything. One has to let go of clinging to all things in order to center wholly in God.

No Way

I should like to persuade spiritual persons that the road leading to God does not entail a multiplicity of considerations, methods, manners and experiences, though these are requirements for beginners. God demands only the one thing necessary: true letting go and letting be through surrender of self both to suffering for Christ and to emptiness in all things. One makes progress only through imitation of Christ Who is the Way, the Truth and the Life. No one goes to the Father but through Him. (Jn 14:6)

One must choose the way that will bring union with God. If a person wants to reach a city, it is necessary to take that road which leads to the city.

If fire is to be united with a log of wood, it is necessary for heat, the means, to prepare the log first with a certain likeness and proportion to the fire. This is done by communicating to the wood a particular amount of heat. Now if anyone wanted to prepare the log by an inadequate means, such as air, water, or earth, there would be no possibility of union between the log and the fire, just as it would be impossible to reach the city without taking the proper road which leads to it.

Everything the intellect can understand, the will experience, and the imagination picture is most unlike and disproportionate to God.

In order to draw near the divine ray the intellect must advance by unknowing rather than by the desire to know, and by blinding itself and remaining in darkness rather than by opening its eyes.

Ray Of
Darkness

Contemplation, by which the intellect has a deeper knowledge of God, is called mystical theology, meaning the secret wisdom of God. This wisdom is secret to the intellect that receives it. Contemplation is a ray of darkness.

There is no ladder among all created, knowable things by which the intellect can reach this Lord.

One can have visions, hear special words, smell fragrances, experience exquisite tastes, and feel touched in an intensely delightful way. However, one must never rely on these feelings through the senses, or accept them but rather flee from them, and have no desire to determine whether they are good or bad.

In so striving to discern, one might forget faith and follow after these communications, believing that their light is the guide and means to the goal, union with God. These feelings of the senses, if they have a divine origin, produce their effect in the spirit at the very moment of perception, without allowing any deliberation about wanting or not wanting them. The divine communications penetrate the soul, move the will to love, and leave their effect within. The soul, even if it wants to, can no more resist them than can a window withstand the light shining on it.

Meditation is the work of the imagination and fantasy

faculties, since it is a discursive act built upon forms, figures and images, imagined and fashioned by the senses.

Three Signs

The soul will have to empty itself of these images and leave this sense in darkness if it is to reach divine union. For these images cannot be an adequate, proximate means to God.

Gradually one will understand the suitability and necessity of letting go, at the required time and season, of all the methods, ways, and uses of the imagination. There are signs a person can notice which indicate that the time and season have come when one can journey freely, making use of that loving attentiveness, and discontinuing the journey along the way of reasoning and imagination.

The first sign is the realization that one cannot practice discursive meditation nor receive satisfaction from it as before. Dryness is now the outcome of fixing the senses upon subjects which formerly provided satisfaction

The second sign is an awareness that one is disinclined to fix the imagination or sense faculties upon other particular objects, interior or exterior.

The third and surest sign is that one chooses to remain alone in loving awareness of God, without particular considerations, in interior peace and quiet repose, without the acts and exercises of the intellect, memory and will. One prefers to remain only in the general, loving awareness and knowledge without any particular knowledge or understanding.

One must observe within at least these three signs together in order to leave safely the state of meditation and sense and enter that of contemplation and spirit.

The more habituated one becomes to this calm, the deeper the experience of the general, loving knowledge of God will grow. This knowledge is more enjoyable than all other things because, without the soul's labor, it affords peace, rest, savor and delight.

One is unable to meditate as before because the spirit no longer derives savor and benefit from this exercise. The moment prayer begins, the soul, as one with a store of water, drinks peaceably, without the labor and need of fetching the water through the channels of past considerations, forms, and figures.

To force a person back to meditation resembles the experience of a sucking child who finds that the breast is taken away just when it is beginning to taste the milk there. As a result the child must renew its efforts.

The Ray Of Light
And The Window

At the moment the soul recollects itself in the presence of God, it enters upon an act of general, loving, peaceful, and tranquil knowledge, drinking wisdom and love and delight.

In observing a ray of sunlight stream through a window, we notice that the more it is pervaded with particles of dust, the clearer and more palpable and sensible it appears to the senses. Yet obviously the sun ray is itself less pure, clear, simple, and perfect in that it is full of so many specks of dust. We also notice that when it is purified of these specks of dust, it seems more obscure to the physical eyes; and the purer it is, the more obscure and incomprehensible it seems to be.

If the ray of sunlight should be entirely cleansed and purified of dust particles, even those most minute, it would not even be visible to the eye, since visible things, the object of the sense of sight, would be absent.

This loving knowledge, like the ray of sunlight, is even at times the cause of darkness, because it takes from the intellect its customary lights, forms, and fantasies.

When one prays with loving attention to God, there is a union with pure love. Time seems to disappear. This is the short prayer which pierces the heavens. It is short because it is not subject to time and it penetrates the heavens because the soul is united with heavenly knowledge. When the individual returns to an awareness of self, the effects this knowledge produced within are evident without the person having been aware of this.

Blessings Of
Loving Attention

The effects are an openness of the mind to heavenly knowledge, and a withdrawal and letting go of all objects, forms, and figures, even of the remembrance of them. One will not fail to understand more or less, being occupied with this knowledge, for there will be an awareness of the delight of love, without particular knowledge of what is loved. As a result this is called a general, loving knowledge.

When one cannot meditate, one should learn to remain in God's presence with a loving attraction and a tranquil intellect, even though the soul seems to be idle.

Learn to be empty of all things, interiorly and exteriorly, and then behold your God.

Guidance

One's spiritual director should receive knowledge of whatever comes through supernatural means for the following reasons: There is not complete confirmation in a soul of the light, strength, and security of many divine communications until they are discussed with a spiritual judge God has destined for this. A soul needs instruction pertinent to its experiences in order to be guided through the dark night to spiritual emptiness and poverty. For the sake of humility and letting go, one should give an account of the experience.

Since God is leading the person by these means, there is no reason for opposing it, nor for becoming frightened or scandalized over it. The director should instead be kind and peaceful, encourage the person and listen to the experience.

Spiritual directors should explain how one act done in charity is more precious in God's sight than all these visions and communications.

It is necessary to base the love and joy of life not upon what is seen or felt but upon God who is transcendent and incomprehensible. That is why our journey toward God must proceed through the negation of all. A person's attitude toward gifts of knowledge should be one of acceptance and humility. For if an experience fails to engender humility, charity, letting go, simplicity, and silence, of what use is it?

The soul must journey to God by knowing God through what God is not, rather than by knowing what God is.

As with the intellect and faith, the soul must draw its memory away from its natural props and capacities and open itself to supreme hope in the incomprehensible God. The memory is without form, figure, or fantasy when united to God, and in great forgetfulness, without the remembrance of anything.

In the beginning a person whose memory is absorbed in God will forget natural things. Yet if the habit of union is present one performs reasonable works and none that are not so. For God's spirit makes one know what must be known and ignore what must be ignored, remember what must be remembered and forget what ought to be forgotten, love what ought to be loved and not love what is not God. The faculties are transformed into divine being.

The Gift
Of Peace

The soul should remain closed without cares or afflictions.
For as Christ entered the room of His disciples bodily, through
closed doors, and gave them peace, He will enter the soul
spiritually, once it has closed the doors of its intellect,
memory, and will to all apprehensions. God will fill the soul
with peace, descending upon it like a river of peace. In this
peace God will remove all misgivings, suspicions, disturbances,
darknesses that made the soul fear it had gone astray. The
soul should persevere in prayer and should hope in the
midst of nakedness and emptiness, for its blessings will
not be long in coming.

Disturbances never arise in a soul unless through the
apprehensions of the memory. When all things are forgotten,
nothing disturbs the peace or stirs the appetite. As the saying
goes: What the eye doesn't see, the heart doesn't want.

Living In Hope

As often as distinct ideas, forms, and images occur, immediately without resting in them, turn to God with loving affection emptied of everything rememberable. Do not think or look upon these things for a longer time than is sufficient for understanding and fulfilling one's obligations.

Consider ideas without clinging to them or seeking fulfillment in them. One is not required to cease recalling and thinking about what one must do and know, for since there is no attachment to the possession of these thoughts, no harm will be done.

We would achieve nothing by emptying intellect and memory in order to ground them in the virtues of faith and hope if we neglected the emptying of the will through charity.

Living A
Passionate Life

The will rules the strength of the soul. When the will directs the faculties, passions, and appetites toward God, turning them away from all that is not God, the soul preserves its strength for God and comes to love God with all its might.

There are four feelings or passions which direct the soul toward God. These are joy, hope, sorrow, and fear. When they are in right order, the individual rejoices only in what is purely for God's honor and glory, hopes for nothing else, feels sorrow only about matters pertaining to this, and fears only God.

The less strongly one fixes the will on God, and the more it is dependent on creatures, the more these four passions combat the soul and reign in it. It then very easily finds joy in what deserves no rejoicing, hope in what brings no profit, sorrow over what perhaps should cause rejoicing, and fear where there is no reason for fear.

When Darkness Descends

*Learn to be empty
of all things, interiorly
and exteriorly, and you
will behold your God*

God
Our Mother

Souls begin to enter this dark night when God, gradually drawing them out of the way of those who practice meditation, begins to give them the gift of contemplation so they might reach divine union.

After it has been resolutely converted to his service, God nurtures and caresses the soul like a loving mother who warms her child with the heat of her bosom, nurses it with good milk and tender food, and carries and caresses it in her arms. But as the child grows older, the mother withholds her caresses and hides her tender love. She rubs bitter aloes on her sweet breast and sets the child down from her arms, letting it walk on its own feet so that it may put aside the habits of childhood and grow accustomed to greater and more important things.

The grace of God acts just like a loving mother by re-engendering in the soul new enthusiasm and fervor in the service of God. With no effort on the soul's part, this grace causes it to taste sweet and delectable milk and to experience intense satisfaction in the performance of spiritual exercises, because God is handing the breast of His tender love to the soul, just as if it were a delicate child.

A number of beginners are plagued by spiritual lust. It happens frequently, in one's very spiritual exercises and without being able to avoid it, that impure movements will be experienced in the sensory part of the soul, and even sometimes when the spirit is deep in prayer or when receiving the sacrament of the Eucharist. These impure feelings arise from three causes outside one's power: from the pleasure human nature finds in spiritual exercises, from the devil, and from fear of these feelings.

Spiritual affection

Some will acquire a liking for other individuals which often arises from lust rather than from the spirit. The affection is purely spiritual if the love of God grows when it grows, or if the love of God is remembered as often as the affection is remembered, or if the affection gives the soul a desire for God.

Like a child withdrawn from the mother's sweet breast, beginners become peevish in the works they do, easily angered by the least thing, and occasionally so unbearable that nobody can put up with them. They are angry over their imperfections and want to become saints in a day. This attitude is contrary to spiritual meekness and can only be remedied by the purgation of the dark night.

The Seven
Vices

The work of beginners is like that of weak children. In acting like children their deeds reflect seven capital vices. Yet others act in an entirely different manner with a different quality of spirit. The first group feels so fervent that a certain kind of secret pride is generated. They strive to impress others when speaking of spiritual things, and in their hearts condemn others who do not seem to have the devotion they want them to have. They dislike praising anyone, but love to receive praise.

Those who have a true spirit act for God humbly and tranquilly and long to be taught by anyone who might help them. They rejoice when others receive praise, and their only sorrow is that they do not serve God as others do.

true spirit of God

Sometimes beginners also possess great spiritual avarice. They become unhappy owing to the lack of the consolations they desire to have in spiritual things. They never have enough of hearing counsels, learning them, keeping them or reading books about them.

Those who are well guided from the outset do not become attached to visible instruments nor burden themselves with them. Their eyes are fixed only upon God, upon being God's friend and pleasing God. This is what they long for.

No matter how excellent their conduct, hardly anyone

among beginners will be spared the fall into spiritual gluttony. This is part of the delight beginners find in their spiritual exercises. Their only yearning and satisfaction is to do what they feel inclined to do. They are eager to receive communion, and in communicating they spend all their time trying to get some feeling and satisfaction rather than humbly praising their God dwelling within.

God often withdraws sensory delight so souls might set the eyes of faith upon the invisible grace God gives in communion. Not only in receiving communion but in other exercises beginners desire to feel God and taste of God as though God was comprehensible and accessible. This desire is a serious imperfection and, because it involves impurity of faith, is opposed to God's way.

As for the other two vices, spiritual envy and sloth, beginners have many imperfections. In regard to envy, they feel sad about the spiritual good of others and experience sensible grief in noting that their neighbor is ahead of them. Because of sloth, they subordinate the way of perfection to the pleasure and delight of their own will. Many want God to desire what they want and become sad if they have to desire God's will. They measure God by themselves and not themselves by God.

The Weaning

The imperfections of those who live in the beginner's state show the need there is for God's help. God weans them from the breasts of these gratifications and delights, takes away all the trivialities and childish ways and makes them acquire the virtues by very different means. God introduces beginners into the dark night, during which all of these imperfections are swept away.

"One dark night," which we say is contemplation, causes two kinds of darkness. One night will be sensory, by which the senses are purged and accommodated to the spirit; the other night will be spiritual, by which the spirit is purged and emptied and prepared for union with God through love.

God desires to liberate souls from the exercise of the senses and of discursive meditation, by which they go in search of God so inadequately and with so many difficulties. He leads them into the exercise of the spirit, in which they become capable of a communion with God that is more abundant and freer of imperfections. God does this after beginners have exercised themselves for a short time in the way of virtue and have persevered in meditation and prayer.

It is through the delight and satisfaction beginners experience in prayer that they have let go of clinging to things and have gained some spiritual strength in God.

It is at this time when, in their opinion, the sun of divine favor is shining most brightly on them, that God darkens all this light and closes the door and empties the spring of the sweet spiritual water they were tasting as often and as long as they desired. God leaves them in such darkness that they do not know which way to turn in their discursive imaginings. They cannot advance a step in meditation, as they used to, now that they are engulfed in this night.

When God sees that they have grown a little, God weans them from the sweet breast so that they might be strengthened, lays aside their swaddling bands, and puts them down from the arms that carried them, that they may grow accustomed to walking by themselves. This change is a surprise to them because everything seems to be working in reverse.

There are signs indicating that the darkness is from God. The first is that as these souls do not get satisfaction or consolation from the things of God, they do not get any from creatures either. God does not allow the soul to find sweetness or delight in anything.

The second sign is that the memory ordinarily turns to God solicitously and with painful care, and the soul thinks it is not serving God but turning back, because it is aware of its distaste for the things of God.

A person suffering this dryness and loss of consolation is ordinarily concerned about not serving God. Because of the little satisfaction it finds, the spirit is ready and strong, though the sensory part of the soul is very cast down, slack and feeble in its actions. God transforms the goods and gifts from sense to spirit.

At this time when a person's efforts are of no avail,

God gives a spiritual and delicate peace Its fruit is quiet, solitary, satisfying and peaceful, very different from the sensory consolations of beginners.

The third sign is the powerlessness, in spite of one's efforts, to meditate and to make use of the imagination. God does not communicate through the senses as before, by means of discursive analysis and synthesis of ideas, but communicates through pure spirit by an act of simple contemplation, in which there is no discursive succession of thought.

God does not bring to contemplation all those who purposely exercise themselves in the way of the spirit, not even half. Why? God best knows. As a result, God never completely weans their senses from the breasts of considerations and discursive meditations, except for some short periods and at certain seasons.

SECTION III

The Symphony
Of Love

*Love never reaches perfection
until the lovers are so alike
that one is transfigured
in the other*

From Sense
To Spirit

At the time of the darkness and dryness of this sensory night, God makes the exchange from sense to spirit by withdrawing the soul from the life of the senses and placing it in that of the spirit. God brings it from meditation to contemplation where the soul no longer has the power to work or meditate with its faculties on the things of God.

This causes great suffering because of the fear that one has gone astray. The attitude necessary in this night of the senses is to pay no attention to discursive meditation, since this is not the time for it. Let the soul remain in rest and quiet.

Be content simply with a loving and peaceful attentiveness to God, and live without the concern, without the effort, and without the desire to taste or feel God.

Contemplation is nothing else than a secret and peaceful and loving inflow of God. This inflow, if not hampered, fires the soul in the spirit of love, as expressed in the verse:

> One dark night
> Fired with love's urgent longings

Since God introduces one into this night to purge the senses and unite the sensory part of the soul to the spiritual part by darkening it and causing a cessation of discursive meditation, one gains so many benefits that the departure from the fetters and straits of the senses is considered a sheer grace.

Because of the benefits in this night the soul says it was a sheer grace to have passed through it. So numerous are these benefits that there is rejoicing in heaven.

Food For
The Soul

God has now taken this soul from its swaddling clothes, has ceased to carry it, making it walk alone, is weaning it from the delicate and sweet food of infants, making it eat bread with crust. The soul is beginning to taste the food of the strong.

The first and chief benefit of this dry and dark night of contemplation is the knowledge of self and of one's great needs. One communes with God more respectfully and courteously, unlike the way the beginner behaved in the prosperity of consolation and satisfaction. One learns that the way to the experience and vision of the power of God does not consist in ideas and meditations about God, but that it embodies one's inability to grasp God with ideas or to walk by means of discursive, imaginative meditation.

In the dryness and emptiness of this night, one also develops spiritual humility and frees the self of all the imperfections of pride experienced at the time of consolations and prosperity. From this humility stems love of neighbors, for one will esteem them, not judging them as before, when enjoying an intense fervor that others did not have.

The soul is likewise liberated from spiritual gluttony. In relation to anger, envy, and sloth, the soul, purged in this dryness of appetite, acquires the virtues to which these vices are opposed. Softened and humbled by dryness and hardships and by other temptations and trials in which God exercises the soul in the course of this night, one becomes meek with God, with one's self, and with one's neighbor.

No longer is there impatient anger with one's self and one's faults, nor with one's neighbor's; neither is one displeased or disrespectfully querulous with God for not granting perfection quickly. The envy is a holy envy that desires to imitate others in solid virtue.

In this arid night, solicitude for God and yearnings about serving God increase. Since the sensory breasts gradually dry up, only the anxiety about serving God remains. Having calmed the four passions, joy, sorrow, hope, and fear, through constantly letting go of clinging, and having lulled to sleep the natural sensory appetites, and having achieved harmony in the interior senses by discontinuing discursive operations, the soul says: "My house being now all stilled."

Freedom

When this house of the senses was stilled and put to sleep through this happy night of purgation, the soul went out to journey along the way of the spirit, the way of infused contemplation, in which God pastures and refreshes the soul without any of its own discursive meditation or active help.

As though liberated from a cramped prison cell, in this new state the soul goes about the things of God with much more freedom and satisfaction of spirit and with more abundant interior delight than it did in the beginning, before entering the night of the senses.

Without the work of meditation, the soul readily finds in its spirit, a very serene, loving contemplation and spiritual delight. But, certain needs, aridities, darknesses, and conflicts are felt since one is not perfect yet.

Uprooting

Since the night of the senses could not reach the spirit, imperfections remain in the night of the spirit. The difference between the two nights is like the difference between pulling up roots and cutting off a branch, or rubbing out a fresh stain and an old, deeply embedded one. To reach union with God, the soul must enter the night of the spirit. In this night both the sensory and spiritual parts are emptied and the soul is made to walk in dark and pure faith, proper means to union with God.

This dark night is an inflow of God into the soul called infused contemplation. It cleanses the soul of its habitual ignorances and imperfections, natural and spiritual. God teaches the soul secretly and instructs it in the perfection of love without its doing anything nor understanding how this happens.

Darkness
And Light

Why, if it is a divine light, does the soul call it a dark night? The clearer and more obvious divine things are in themselves, the darker and more hidden they are to the soul naturally. The brighter the light, the more the owl is blinded. The more one looks at the brilliant sun, the more the sun darkens the faculty of sight, deprives it and over-whelms it in its weakness.

The afflictions of this dark night of the spirit are many. One feels helpless as though imprisoned in a dark dungeon, bound hands and feet, and able neither to move, nor see, nor feel any favor from heaven or earth. This condition remains until the spirit is humbled, softened, and purified and until it becomes so delicate, simple, and refined that it can be one with the Spirit of God, according to the degree of union with love that God desires to grant.

To be truly efficacious, this night will last for some years, although there are intervals in which this dark contemplation, ceasing to assail the soul, shines upon it illuminatively and lovingly. Then the soul, like one who has been unshackled and released from a dungeon to enjoy the benefit of spacious-ness and freedom, experiences great sweetness of peace and loving friendship with God in a ready abundance of spiritual communication. This illumination is, for the soul, a sign of the health the darkness is producing in it and a foretaste of the abundance for which it hopes.

Yet the soul does not cease to feel that something is lacking or remaining to be done and this feeling keeps it from fully enjoying the rest. It feels as though an enemy is within who, although pacified and put to sleep, will awaken and cause trouble.

The Cloud
Of Grief

When one feels safest, and least expects it, the darkness returns in a degree more severe than before. A person suffering in this way knows how much he/she loves God and would give a thousand lives for God, yet there is no relief. In loving God so intensely nothing else is of concern and, aware of one's own misery, one is unable to believe in the love of God.

It also seems that God has placed a cloud in front of the soul so that its prayer might not pass through. Consequently, one can neither pray vocally nor be attentive to spiritual matters, and still less attend to temporal affairs and business. The more simply and purely the divine light strikes the soul, the more it darkens and empties it in its affections for both earthly and heavenly things.

Dust In
The Light

If a ray of sunlight should enter through one window, traverse the room, and go out through another window without coming in contact with any object or dust particles on which it could reflect, the room would have no more light than previously and the ray would not be visible.

Instead, there is more darkness where the ray is visible, because it takes away and darkens some of the other light. This ray is invisible because there are no objects on which it can reflect. This is precisely what the divine ray of contemplation does.

This happy night darkens the spirit only to impart light concerning all things. It humbles a person and reveals miseries only to exalt. It impoverishes and empties one of all possessions and natural affection, only that one may reach out to the enjoyment of all earthly and heavenly things with a general freedom of spirit.

The Soul
On Fire

This loving knowledge or divine light we are speaking of has the same effect on a soul that a fire has on a log of wood. The soul is purged and prepared for union with the divine light just as the wood is prepared for transformation into the fire. Fire, when applied to wood, first dehumidifies it, dispelling all moisture and making it give off any water it contains. Then it gradually turns the wood black, makes it dark and ugly, and even causes it to emit a bad odor. By drying out the wood, the fire brings to light and expels all those ugly and dark accidents which are contrary to fire. Finally, by heating and enkindling it from without, the fire transforms the wood into itself and makes it as beautiful as the fire itself.

Once transformed, the wood no longer has any activity or passivity of its own, except for its weight and its quantity which is denser than the fire. It possesses the properties and performs the actions of fire: it is dry and it dries; it is hot and it gives off heat; it is brilliant and it illumines; and it is also light, much lighter than before. It is the fire that produces all these properties in the soul.

This comparison fits many of the things said about the two nights. The very loving light and wisdom into which the soul will be transformed is that which in the beginning purges and prepares it, just as the fire which transforms the wood by incorporating it into itself is that which was first preparing it for this transformation.

Without this purgation the soul cannot receive the divine light, sweetness, and delight of wisdom, just as the log of wood, until prepared, cannot be transformed by the fire that is applied to it.

As the soul is purified by this fire of love, it is further enkindled in love, just as the wood becomes hotter as the fire prepares it. As the fire penetrates more deeply into the wood its action becomes stronger and more vehement, preparing the innermost part in order to gain possession of it.

The fruit of the soul's tears and happy traits is expressed in the verse "fired with love's urgent longings." The soul refers to the fire of love which, like material fire acting on wood, penetrates it in this night of painful contemplation.

This enkindling of love occurs in the spirit, and through it the soul, in the midst of these dark conflicts, feels vividly and keenly that it is being wounded by a strong divine love, and it has a certain feeling and foretaste of God. The spirit experiences an impassioned and intense love, because this spiritual inflowing engenders the passion of love.

Only the love of God which is being united to the soul imparts the heat, strength, and passion of love, or fire, as the soul feels it. This love finds that the soul is equipped to receive the wound and union in the measure that it has let go of clinging to all things. God gathers together all the strength, faculties, and appetites of the soul, spiritual and sensory alike, that the energy and power of this harmonious composite may be employed in this love. The soul arrives at the fulfillment of the first commandment.

Because of the strength of the soul's love and desire, actions are performed without any considerations or concerns. Mary Magdalen illustrates this at the banquet. In spite of her past, she paid no heed to the crowds of men, prominent as well as unknown. She did not consider the appropriateness of weeping and shedding tears in the presence of Our Lord's guests. Her only concern was to reach Him for Whom her soul was already wounded and on fire, without any delay and without waiting for a more opportune time.

Such is the courage of love: even knowing that her Beloved was shut up in the tomb, which was sealed by a huge rock and surrounded by guards so that the disciples could not steal His body, she did not let this keep her from going out before daybreak with ointments to anoint Him.

Finally, this complete and urgent longing of love prompted Mary to ask the man she thought was the gardener if he had stolen Him and, if he had, to tell her where he put Him so that she could take Him away. She did not stop to realize that her question in the light of sound judgment was foolish, for obviously if he had stolen the Lord, he would not have told her, and still less would he have allowed her to take Him away.

Mary's love was so ardent that she thought she would go and take Him away, however great the impediments. Rightly and reasonably does the soul call this

"Ah, the sheer grace!"

The enamored soul must leave its house then in order to reach its goal. It must go out at night when all the members of its house are asleep; that is, when the operations, passions, and appetites of the soul are put to sleep by means of this night. God put them to sleep to enable the soul to go out to the spiritual union of perfect love of God without being seen. Such a person will understand how the life of the spirit is true freedom and wealth and embodies inestimable goods.

The soul is secure when it walks in darkness. God takes a person by the hand and guides the soul in darkness, as though blind, to an unknown place. Past knowledge cannot serve as a guide to reach a new and unknown land and to travel unknown roads.

Faith darkens and empties the intellect of all its natural understanding and thereby prepares it for union with the divine wisdom. Hope empties and withdraws the memory from all creature possessions.

Charity empties and annihilates the affections and appetites of the will of whatever is not God and centers them on God alone.

Using the metaphor and similitude of temporal night to describe this spiritual night, the soul then enumerates and extols the good properties of the night. The first is that in this glad contemplative night, God conducts the soul by so solitary and secret a contemplation that nothing pertinent to the senses, nor any touch of creature, can reach or detain it on the route leading to the union of love.

The second property of this night is the darkness which obscures the faculties so that the soul is free of hindrance from the forms and figures of natural apprehensions which usually prevent it from union with God.

The third property is that love alone, which burns by soliciting the heart for the Beloved, is what guides and moves it and makes it soar to God in an unknown way along the road of solitude, "on that glad night."

Seeking
The Beloved

Oh, soul, most beautiful among all creatures, so anxious to know the dwelling place of your Beloved that you may go in quest of the Bridegroom and be united with him, we tell you that you yourself are the dwelling, secret chamber, and hiding place. "Behold the kingdom of God is within you." (Lk 17:21) Do not go outside yourself in pursuit of your Beloved.

You ask, "Since He whom my soul loves is within me, why don't I find or experience him?" The Beloved is concealed. Your Bridegroom is like a treasure hidden in a field, for which the merchant sold all his possessions (Mt 13:44), and that field is your soul. In order to find Him you should forget all your possessions and creatures and hide in the interior, secret chambers of your spirit. And there, closing the door behind you, you should pray to your Father in secret. (Mt 6:6)

Remaining hidden with Him, you will experience Him in hiding, love and enjoy Him in hiding. You will delight with Him in hiding, that is, in a way transcending all language and feeling. Do not be like many foolish ones who think that when they do not understand, taste, or experience God, that God is far away and utterly concealed. Nothing is obtained from God except by love.

When the soul cannot converse with her loved one, she does so through the best means possible. Her desires, affections, and moanings are messengers that know how to manifest to the Beloved the secret of the lover's heart.

The soul knows that not all needs and petitions reach the point at which God, in hearing, grants them. They must wait until, in God's eyes, they arrive at the suitable time, season, and number and then God sees and hears them. Every soul should know that even though God does not answer its prayer immediately, God will not on that account fail to answer it at the opportune time if the soul does not become discouraged and give up its prayer.

The soul is aware that neither her sighs and prayers nor the help of good intermediaries are sufficient for her to find her Beloved. Since the desire in which she seeks the Beloved is authentic and her love intense, she does not want to leave any possible means untried. She desires to look for the Beloved through her works. She must practice the virtues, engaging in the spiritual exercises of the active and contemplative life.

The soul decides to go out searching for the Beloved, seeking Him through works so that she may not be left without finding Him. Many desire that God cost them no more than words. They scarcely desire to do anything for Him that might cost them something. Yet, unless they go in search of God, seeking God through works, they will not find Him, no matter how much they cry for Him.

The soul has made known the manner of preparing oneself to begin this journey in the practice of self-knowledge, the first requirement for advancing to the knowledge of

Traces
Of God

God created all things with remarkable ease and brevity, and in them He left some trace of Who He is, not only in giving all things being from nothing but even by endowing them with innumerable graces and qualities, making them beautiful in a wonderful order and unfailing dependence on one another. All of this He did through His own wisdom, the Word, His only begotten Son by whom He created them.

The creatures are like a trace of God's passing. Through them one can track down God's grandeur, might, wisdom, and other divine attributes. In the redemption of all things through the Incarnation of God's Son and through the glory of His resurrection, the Father clothed creatures wholly in beauty and dignity.

In the living contemplation and knowledge of creatures, the soul sees the fullness of grace, power, and beauty with which God has endowed them that seemingly all are arranged in wonderful beauty and natural virtue. This beauty and virtue are derived from God and imparted by that infinite super-natural beauty of the image of God. God's look clothes the world and all the heavens with beauty and gladness.

The soul says: You have communicated by means of others, as if joking with me; now may You truly grant me a communication of Yourself, by Yourself. Instead of other messengers, may You then be both the messenger and message.

Corresponding to three kinds of knowledge there exist three ways of suffering for the Beloved.

The first is a wound coming from one's knowledge of creatures. The second is a sore wound coming from knowledge of the Incarnation and the mysteries of the faith. The third is like dying, an impatient love, making the soul live the life of love, transforming her in love. The soul prays for healing:

> "Why, since you wounded
> This heart, don't you heal it?
> And why, since you stole it from me,
> Do you leave it so,
> And fail to carry off what you have
> stolen?"

The lover asks the Beloved why He has not taken her heart away since it has been stolen. This leaves the soul like an empty vessel waiting to be filled, or a hungry man craving for food or a sick person moaning for health. Such is the truly loving heart.

God grants a certain spiritual feeling of His presence to the loving soul whose prayers are so enkindled and who seeks God more covetously than one seeks money. As one throws water into the forge to stir up the fire, so the Lord usually grants to some souls who walk in the longings of love certain signs of excellence to prepare them for greater gifts.

With the same evenness of soul, true love receives all things that come from the Beloved: prosperity, adversity, even chastisement.

The Cure

The lover experiences the sickness of love cured only by God's presence. The reason for love-sickness is that love of God is the soul's health. When one possesses some degree of love of God, no matter how small, she is alive, yet weak and infirm because of her little love. In the measure that love increases she will be healthier and when love is perfect she will have full health.

Love never reaches perfection until the lovers are so alike that one is transfigured in the other.

The soul striving to love God in this way feels that she is rushing toward God as impetuously as a falling stone, or as wax in which an impress is being made, but not yet completed. She also feels like a sketch of a drawing and calls out to the one who did the sketch to finish the painting. She turns again to faith in her longing for love.

Faith is that which most vividly sheds light covering her Beloved so that she takes it as a means toward union. She has the truths of faith sketched deep within her, in her intellect and will. Over the sketch of faith is drawn, in the will of the lover, the sketch of love.

The Void
Of God

Yet she still suffers because she is drawing nearer to God and so has greater experience within herself of the void of God. God sends the soul suffering some of the divine rays with such strong love and glory she goes out of herself completely.

God's favors and visits are generally in accord with the intensity of the yearnings and ardors of love which precede them. From natural fear the soul tells the Beloved to withdraw the visits of love; yet no matter what the cost, she would not want to lose the visits and favors of the Beloved.

As a breeze cools and refreshes a person worn from the heat, God sends a breeze of love refreshing and renewing the soul burning with the fire of love. God does not place the gift of grace and love in the soul except according to its desires and love. Anyone truly loving God must strive not to fail in this love. This will induce God to love and delight in the person. The soul must practice what St. Paul taught:

"Charity is patient, is kind, is not envious, does no evil, does not become proud, is not ambitious, seeks not its own, does not become disturbed, thinks no evil, rejoices not in iniquity, but rejoices in truth, suffers all things, believes all things, hopes all things and endures all things." (1 Cor 13:4-7)

From this recollection the soul finds all that she desired is inexpressible. She praises her Beloved.

All Things
Are In God

My beloved is the mountains,
And lovely wooded valleys
Strange islands,
And resounding rivers
The whistling of love-stirring breezes

The tranquil night
At the time of the rising dawn
Silent music,
Sounding solitude
The supper that refreshes, and
     deepens love

After much spiritual exercise, God places the soul in the union of love called spiritual espousal with the Word, the Son of God. God communicates to the soul great things. Not only do the yearning and complaints of love cease, but also a feeling of peace, delight, and gentleness of love begins in her.

She no longer speaks of sufferings and longings as before, but of the communion of sweet and peaceful love with her Beloved, because now all those sufferings have ceased. Inasmuch as the soul is united with God she feels that all things are God as St. John expressed in the words: "That which was made had life in Him." (Jn 1:4)

In this spiritual sleep in the bosom of the Beloved, the soul possesses the tranquility, rest, and quietude of the peaceful night. She receives in God, together with this peace, a fathomless and obscure divine knowledge. The tranquil night is not equivalent to a dark night, but rather, it is like the night at the time of rising dawn. Just as the night at the rise of dawn is not entirely night or entirely day, so this divine solitude and tranquillity has some share in the divine light but not its complete clarity.

In that nocturnal tranquility and silence and in that knowledge of the divine light, the soul becomes aware of Wisdom's wonderful harmony and sequence in the variety of God's creatures and works. Each of them is endowed with a certain likeness of God and in its own way gives voice to who God is. Creatures will be for the soul a harmonious symphony of sublime music because in the Beloved she knows and enjoys the symphony of silent music.

It is also sounding solitude because when the spiritual faculties are alone and empty in all natural forms and apprehensions, they can receive in a most sonorous way the spiritual sound of the excellence of God in all creatures. All the praise of God from creatures is like music, for each one possesses God's gifts differently, each one sings God's praises differently and all of them together form a symphony of love, as of music.

According to what each in itself has received from God, the soul perceives in that tranquil wisdom that all creatures raise their voices in testimony to what God is. She beholds that each in its own way, bearing God within itself according to its capacity, magnifies God. And thus all these voices form one voice of music praising the grandeur, wisdom, and wonderful knowledge of God.

The lover enjoys with her Beloved the supper that refreshes and deepens love. Just as supper comes at the end of a day's work and at the beginning of the evening rest, this tranquil knowledge causes the soul to experience a certain end of her evils and the possession of good things in which her love of God is deepened more than before.

Espousal

The soul begins to feel that the Beloved is in her as in His own bed. She offers herself together with her virtues, like flowers in her garden, which she can render to the Beloved. Desirous that neither the envious and malicious devils, nor the wild sensory appetites, nor the wanderings of the imagination, nor any other knowledge or awareness keep this interior delight of love, which is the flower of her vineyard, the bride wakes the angels. She tells them to catch all these disturbances, the foxes, and keep them from interfering with the interior exercise of love, in the delight of which the virtues and graces are communicated and enjoyed by the soul and the Son of God.

The soul feels that these virtues are both in her and in God so that they seem to form a flowering and pleasant vineyard belonging to the Bridegroom and to herself and in which they both feed and delight. She offers a bouquet to the Beloved. She prays that there will be no one to appear on the hill, that is, no particular knowledge or affection or other considerations of the memory, intellect or will; and no other digressions, forms, images, or figures of objects, or other natural operations in any of the bodily senses or faculties, either interior or exterior.

The soul still experiences the absence of God and since

she has a singular and intense love of God, the absence is a torment for her.

She asks the Holy Spirit to breathe through her garden, to touch it, to put in motion the virtues already given, renewing them and moving them to offer a wonderful fragrance and sweetness. She knows the Bridegroom communicates with the soul by means of the virtues, feeds on the soul transforming her into Himself, now that she is prepared.

The Holy Spirit guides her so that she will become an open door to the Bridegroom that he may enter through the complete and true "yes" of love, the yes of espousal. The four passions of the soul, joy, hope, sorrow, and fear, are calmed by the Beloved. He does this so that they may cease not only to reign in her but also not to cause her any displeasure.

She no longer has the feeling of compassion, even though she possesses its work and perfection. The soul is transformed, like the woman who, having lit the candle and hunted through her whole house for the lost drachma, is holding it up in her hands with gladness and calling to her friends and neighbors to come and celebrate. (Lk 15:8-9) Now, too, that the soul is liberated, this loving shepherd and Bridegroom rejoices.

The Bridegroom calls the soul His crown, His bride, and the joy of His heart, and takes her now in his arms and goes forth with her. In calling the soul His bride, He tells her she has reached the state of spiritual marriage.

Spiritual Marriage

The spiritual marriage is incomparably greater than the spiritual espousal, for it is a total transformation in the Beloved in which each surrenders the entire possession of self to the other with a certain consummation of the union of love. The soul thereby becomes divine, becomes God through participation, insofar as is possible in this life.

There are two natures in one spirit and love. This union resembles the union of the light of a star or candle with the light of the sun, for what sheds light is not the star or candle, but the sun, which has absorbed the other lights into its own.

The soul has been transformed into her God, "the sweet garden," because of the sweet and pleasant dwelling she finds in Him. One does not reach this garden of full transformation, which is the joy, delight, and glory of spiritual marriage, without first passing through the spiritual espousal and the loyal and mutual love of betrothed persons.

For after the soul has been for some time the betrothed of the Son of God in gentle and complete love, God calls her and places her in His flowering garden to consummate this most joyful state of marriage with Him. The union wrought between these two natures and the communication of the divine to the human are such that even though neither changes their being, both appear to be God.

Following
The Footprints

The soul that has arrived at the spiritual marriage is not content with enjoying the excellence of her Beloved, the Son of God, nor in rendering thanks for favors and delights from Him. She also praises and thanks Him for the favors bestowed on others. She praises the "footprints" of God, the traces of God found in all things.

A person's footprints are the traces by which one can track that person. God's sweetness and knowledge, given to the soul who seeks God, are the traces by which she goes on knowing and searching. Following God's footprints, souls run along the way by external practice and works. Then there are interior experiences of the will moved by favors, the "touch of a spark" and "special wine."

The touch of a spark is a very subtle spark which the Beloved sometimes produces in a soul and which inflames in her the fire of love as if a hot spark were to leap from the fire and set her ablaze. The special wine is a favor in which God inebriates the soul in the Holy Spirit with a wine of sweet, delightful, fortified love.

The soul arrives at the inner wine cellar, the last and most intimate degree of love in which the soul can be placed in this life. There are seven degrees or wine cellars of love. They are all possessed when the seven gifts of the Holy Spirit are possessed perfectly according to the soul's capacity for receiving them.

Few in this life reach the last and most perfect wine cellar, the spiritual marriage, the perfect union with God. What God communicates is totally beyond words.

In this transformation the two become one, as we would say of the window united with the ray of sunlight, or of the coal with fire, or of the starlight with the light of the sun. One can say "I drank of my Beloved."

As the drink is diffused through all the members of the body, so this communication is diffused substantially through the whole soul. With the intellect she drinks wisdom and knowledge; with the will, sweetest love; and with the memory she drinks refreshment and delight in the remembrance and the feeling of glory.

In this interior union God communicates with the soul with such genuine love that no mother's affection in which she tenderly caresses her child, nor brother's love, nor friendship is comparable to it. God is occupied here in favoring and caressing the soul like a mother who ministers to her child and nurses it at her breast.

The soul knows the truth of Isaiah's words: "You shall be carried at the breast of God and upon God's knees you will be caressed." (Is 66:12)

The bride says: "There He gave me His breast — and I gave myself to Him keeping nothing back." Giving one's breast to another signifies the giving of love and friendship to another and the revealing of secrets to another as to a friend. When the bride says that there He gave her his breast, she means that He communicated His love and secrets to her there.

Like the bee that extracts honey from all the wildflowers and will not use them for anything else, the soul easily extracts the sweetness of love from all the things that happen to her; that is, she loves God in them. Thus everything leads her to love as she says, "Now that my every act is love."

It should be noted that until the soul reaches this state of union of love she should practice love in both the active and contemplative life. The soul cannot acquire or practice the virtues without the help of God. By continuing in prayer and efforts the soul may one day, like the bride, "weave garlands" for the Beloved.

The Look
Of Love

By means of garlands, interwoven and placed in the soul, the bride wishes to describe the divine union of love between herself and God. The flowers represent the Bridegroom. The soul's love is what unites and fastens her to this flower of flowers. The thread of love joins and binds God and the soul so strongly that it unites and transforms them.

The bride quickly acknowledges that all is accomplished by the look of love from her Beloved. The reason she captivated the Beloved and the eye of her faith wounded Him was that He favored her by looking at her with love. By this look of love He made her gracious and pleasing to Him. For the soul the power to look at God is the power to do works in the grace of God.

The soul explains "She lives in solitude — and in solitude He guides her."

Strange it is, this property of lovers, that they like to enjoy one another's companionship alone, apart from every other creature and all company. If some stranger is present, they do not enjoy each other fully. The reason they desire to commune with each other alone is that love is a union between the two alone.

The soul desires to see herself further within God. She wants to enter "into the thicket," the splendid works and judgments of God and the thicket of trials and tribulations that bring her deep into the wisdom of God. Suffering is the means of her penetrating further into the delectable wisdom of God.

Transformation

She desires to breathe the air of God and receives the breathlike spiration, the Holy Spirit, who expands the soul sublimely and informs her. This makes her capable of breathing in God the same spiration of love that the Father breathes in the Son and the Son in the Father. This is the Holy Spirit, Who in the Father and Son breathes out to her in this transformation in order to unite her to them.

That which comes to pass in this communication is unspeakable, for the soul united and transformed in God, breathes out in God to God the very divine spiration which God — she being transformed in Him — breathes out to her. The soul possesses the same good by participation that the Son possesses by nature. As a result souls are truly gods by participation, equal to and companions of God.

The bride sets all this perfection and preparedness before her Beloved, the Son of God, with the desire that He transfer from the spiritual marriage, to which He desired to bring her in this Church Militant, to the glorious marriage of the Triumphant.

May the most sweet Jesus, Bridegroom of faithful souls, be pleased to bring all who evoke his name to this glorious marriage.

Transformation In The Beloved

*God's look clothes
the world and all the heavens
with beauty and gladness*

Transforming Fire

Why marvel at God who grants such sublime and strange gifts? Jesus declared that the Father, Son, and the Holy Spirit would take up their abode in anyone who loved Him. (Jn 14:23) The "living flame of love" is about love in the state of transformation that has a deeper quality and is more perfect.

It resembles the activity of fire. Although the fire has penetrated the wood, transformed it, and united it with itself, yet as the fire grows hotter and continues to burn, the wood becomes much more incandescent and inflamed, even to the point of flaring up and shooting out flames from itself.

The soul is so inwardly transformed in the fire of love and has received such quality from it that it is not merely united to the fire but produces within it a living flame.

This flame of love is the Spirit of the Bridegroom, who is the Holy Spirit.

The living flame of love is a flame of divine life and wounds the soul with the tenderness of divine life. It wounds and stirs it so deeply as to make it dissolve in love. It is something splendid that, since love is never idle but in continued motion, it is always emitting flames everywhere like a blazing fire.

The soul feels it "in its deepest center." The soul's center is God. When it has revealed God with all its capacity of being and strength, it will have attained to its final and deepest center in God. It will know, love, and enjoy God with all its might.

The more degrees of love the soul has, the more deeply it enters into God and centers itself in God. There are as many centers in God possible to the soul, each one deeper than the other, as there are degrees of love possible to it. These are the many mansions the Son of God declared were in His Father's house. (Jn 14:2)

It should not be held as incredible in a soul examined, purged, and tried in the fire of tribulations, trials, and temptations and found faithful in love, that the promise of the Son of God be fulfilled, that the Most Blessed Trinity will come and dwell within anyone who loves God. (Jn 14:23) The Blessed Trinity inhabits the soul by divinely illumining the intellect with the wisdom of the Son, delighting its will in the Holy Spirit, and by absorbing it powerfully and mightily in the delightful embrace of the Father's sweetness.

This activity of the Holy Spirit is something far greater than what occurs in the communication and transformation of love. The two kinds of union, union of love alone and union with an inflowing love, are comparable to the fire of God and the furnace of God. The one signifies the Church Militant in which the fire of charity is not completely kindled; the other the vision of peace, the Church Triumphant, where this fire is like a furnace blazing in the perfection of love.

The Holy Spirit sets in motion the glorious flickerings of His flame. The very fire of love which afterwards is united with the soul, glorifying it, is that which previously assails it by purifying it, just as the fire that penetrates a log of wood is the same fire that first makes an assault upon it, wounding it, drying it out and stripping it of the unsightly qualities until it is so disposed that it can be penetrated and transformed into the fire.

Veils
Of God

The flame previously oppressed the soul in an inde-
scribable way, since contraries were battling contraries: God,
Who is all perfect against all the imperfections of the soul.
God does this, that by transforming the soul into Himself,
He might soften, pacify and clarify it as does fire when it
penetrates the wood.

The soul petitions: "Tear through the veil of this sweet
encounter." There are three veils which constitute a hindrance
to this union with God, and which must be torn if the union
is to be effected and possessed perfectly by the soul. They
are the temporal veil, comprising all creatures; the natural
veil, embodying the purely natural inclinations and operations;
and the sensitive veil which consists only of the union of
the soul with the body.

The first two veils must necessarily be torn in order to
obtain this union with God in which all things of the world
are let go, all the natural appetites and affections mortified,
and the natural operations of the soul divinized.

All of this was accomplished, and these veils were torn
by means of the oppressive encounters of this flame. Through
the spiritual purgation described in the "Dark Night" and
the "Ascent" the soul tears these two veils completely and
is united with God, as it now is. Only the third veil of this

sensitive life remains to be torn. Because the veil is now so tenuous, thin and spiritualized through this union with God, the flame is not harsh in its encounter as it was with the other two, but a "sweet encounter." It seems about to tear through the veil of mortal life.

The deaths of such persons are very gentle and very sweet, sweeter and more gentle than were their whole spiritual lives on earth.

The soul proclaims how the three Persons of the Most Blessed Trinity, the Father, the Son, and the Holy Spirit, are they who effect in it this divine union. "O sweet cautery, O delightful wound! O gentle hand! O delicate touch." The cautery is the Holy Spirit, the hand is the Father, the touch is the Son. The gift of transformation, a gift by which all debts are paid, is the gift of the Trinity to the soul.

The soul feels this union in its deepest center. It is a soul on fire with love.

The soul inflamed with love of God will feel that a seraphim is assailing it by means of an arrow or dart which is all afire with love. The seraphim pierces and cauterizes the soul which, like a red hot coal, or better a flame, is already enkindled. And in this cauterization, when the soul is transpierced with a dart, the flame gushes forth, vehemently and with a sudden ascent, like the fire in a furnace or an oven when someone uses a poker or bellows to stir and excite it.

The soul feels its ardor strengthen and increase. Its love becomes so refined that seemingly there are seas of loving fire within it, reaching to the heights and depths of the earthly and heavenly spheres, imbuing all with love.

It seems to the soul that the entire universe is a sea of love in which it is engulfed, for, conscious of the living point or center of love within itself, it is unable to catch sight of the boundaries of this love.

The soul "tastes of eternal life." It tastes all the things of God, since God communicates to it fortitude, wisdom, love, beauty, grace, and goodness. It also feels the truth of "pays every debt." It feels the reward for the trials it passed through in order to reach this state.

It ought to be pointed out why there are so few who reach this union with God. The reason is not God's wish that there be only a few. God would rather want all to be perfect, but finds few vessels that will endure so sublime a work.

God tries them in little things and finds them so weak that they immediately flee from work, unwilling to be subject to the least discomfort and not wanting to let go of attachments. It follows that, not finding them strong and faithful in that little (Mt 25:21-23) in which God favored them by beginning to hew and polish them, He realized that they will be less strong in greater trials and proceeds no further in purifying them.

Such souls, unwilling to suffer trials, shun them, flee from the narrow road of life, and seek the broad road of their own consolation. Thus they do not allow God to begin to grant their petition for advancing. Those who do suffer with patience come to share the consolations as they shared in the suffering.

The soul realizes and says to God: "In killing, You changed death to life." Spiritually speaking there are two kinds of life: beatific, consisting in the vision of God, which must be attained by death; and the perfect spiritual life, the possession of God through the union of love. This is acquired through complete letting go of all the vices and appetites of one's own nature.

In this experience of death the soul, like a true child of God, is moved in all by the Spirit of God. Accordingly, the intellect of this soul is God's intellect; the will is God's will; its memory is its memory of God; its delight is God's delight. Although the substance of the soul is not the substance of God, since it cannot undergo a substantial conversion into God, it has become God through participation in God, being united to and absorbed in God.

Lamps
Of Fire

The soul rejoices because from the splendors and love it receives it can shine brightly in the presence of its spouse and gives Him love through its "lamps of fire." These lamps transmit both light and heat; they shine and burn within the soul. The soul, like God, gives forth light and warmth through each of God's attributes. God is for the soul many lamps together. These illumine and impart warmth to it individually, for it has clear knowledge of each of God's attributes, and through this knowledge enkindles in love.

When one loves and does good to another, one loves and does good in the measure of one's own nature and properties. Thus, the soul's Bridegroom, dwelling within it, grants favors according to His nature. Since the Bridegroom is omnipotent, He omnipotently loves and does good to it. Since He is wise, good, holy, just, merciful, one feels that He loves and does good in one with wisdom, goodness, holiness, justice, mercy. Since He is a strong, sublime, and delicate being, one feels His love in this way. Since He is pure and truthful, one feels that He loves in a pure and truthful way.

Who will be able to express this experience? The soul at this time is flooded with divine waters, abounding in them like a plentiful font overflowing on all sides.

The fire from the lamps is so gentle and immense it is like the waters of life, which satisfy the thirst of the spirit with that impetus the spirit desires. The lamps of fire are living waters of the spirit.

All that can be said now is less than the reality, for the transformation of the soul in God is indescribable. This can express everything: the soul becomes God from God through participation in God and God's attributes, which it terms "lamps of fire."

God is always wanting to bestow eternal life and transport the soul completely to eternal glory. All the gifts, first and last, great and small, which God grants to the soul, are granted in order to lead it to eternal life.

In the same way the flame flickers and flares together with the enkindled air in order to bring the air with itself to the center of the sphere. It produces all these movements in order to persist in bringing the air nearer itself. As the flame does not carry the air away because the air is in its own sphere, so too, although these movements of the Holy Spirit are most efficacious in absorbing the soul in glory, they do not do so completely until the time comes for it to depart from the sphere of the air of this life and enter into the center of the spirit of the perfect life in Christ.

These lamps are also called overshadowings. An overshadowing is the equivalent of casting a shadow. Casting a shadow is similar to protecting, favoring, and granting graces.

Shadows
Of God

When a shadow covers a person, it is a sign that someone else is nearby to protect and favor that person. The Angel Gabriel called the conception of the Son of God, that favor granted to the Virgin Mary, an overshadowing of the Holy Spirit. (Lk 1:35)

The shadow that the lamp of God's attributes casts over the soul will be the very wisdom, beauty, and fortitude of God in shadow, because the soul here cannot comprehend God perfectly.

The shadows of the lamps of God's attributes are the deposit of the Father's treasures, the splendor of its eternal light, the unspotted mirror and image of His goodness, "in whose splendors the deep caverns of feeling give forth both warmth and light to their Beloved."

Caverns

The caverns are the soul's faculties: memory, intellect, and will. They are deep and capable of holding boundless goods since anything less than the infinite fails to fill them. From what they suffer when they are empty, we can give some knowledge of their enjoyment and delight when they are filled with God.

The pain of the void of these caverns is worse than death. The void of the intellect is thirst for the waters of God's wisdom, the object of the intellect. The hunger of the will is for the perfection of love which is its aim. The void of the memory is a yearning and a melting away of the soul to be possessed by God. The greater the soul's desire for God to fill the caverns, the greater will be its delight and satisfaction rather than its suffering and pain.

Espousal
And Marriage

There is a difference between the possession of God
through grace and through union, for one lies in loving
and the other also includes communication. The difference
resembles that between betrothal and marriage.

In espousal there is only a mutual agreement and will-
ingness between the two, and the bridegroom graciously
gives jewels to the espoused. But in marriage there is also
a communication and union between the persons. When the
soul has reached purity in itself, and has let go of other
alien satisfactions, rendering its "yes" to God concerning
all of this, then the soul has attained the possession of
God insofar as this is possible by way of the will and grace.
This is a state of intense delight, but the delights are not
comparable to those of marriage.

Three Blind Men

If a person is seeking God, God, the Beloved, is seeking the person much more. There are three blind men who can draw the soul off the road of seeking God: the spiritual director, the devil and the soul itself.

Many spiritual directors cause great harm to a number of souls because, in not understanding the ways and properties of the spirit, they instruct them in the ways of beginners, which the spiritual directors themselves have used or read of somewhere. Knowing no more than this they do not wish souls to pass beyond their beginnings and their discursive and imaginative ways even though God desires to lead them on.

Directors should reflect on these two things: that they are not the chief agent, guide, and mover of souls, but that the principal guide is the Holy Spirit, Who is never neglectful of souls; and that they are instruments for directing souls to perfection through faith and the love of God, according to the spirit God gives each one.

Not everyone who is capable of hewing the wood knows how to carve the statue, nor does everyone able to carve know how to perfect and polish the work, nor do all who know how to polish know how to paint it, nor do all who can paint it know how to put the finishing touches on it and bring it to completion. One can do no more with the statue than one has learned to do, and were an effort made to do more than this the statue would be ruined.

If you are only a hewer, which lies in guiding the soul to let go of the world and of its desires, or a good carver, which consists in introducing it to holy meditation, and know no more, how can you lead the soul to the ultimate perfection of delicate painting, which no longer requires hewing or carving or even polishing and painting but the work God must do in it?

Spiritual directors should give freedom to souls and encourage them in their desire to seek improvement.

The second blind man who is capable of thwarting the soul in this kind of recollection is the devil. The devil tries to intrude in the recollection with some clouds of knowledge and sensible satisfaction.

Since one is inclined toward feeling and tasting, especially if seeking something and not understanding the road travelled, an attachment easily grows for the knowledge and satisfaction provided by the devil and the solitude God was providing is lost.

The devil makes the soul lose abundant riches by alluring it with a little bait, as one would allure a fish, out of the simple waters of the spirit, where it was engulfed and swallowed up in God without finding any bottom or foothold. And by this bait the devil provides, he drags the soul ashore so that it might find the ground and go on foot with great effort, rather than swim in the ocean of God.

The third blind man is the soul which, by not understanding itself, disturbs and harms itself. Since it only knows how to act by means of the senses and discursive reflection, it thinks it is doing nothing when God introduces it into that emptiness and solitude where it is unable to use the faculties. The soul that was enjoying the idleness of spiritual silence and peace, in which God was secretly adorning it, is distracted and filled with dryness and displeasure.

The soul thus resembles a child who kicks and cries in order to walk when his mother wants to carry him, and thus neither allows his mother to make any headway nor makes any himself; or it resembles one who moves a painting back and forth while the artist is at work so that either nothing is accomplished or the painting is damaged.

Participation
In God

Having been made one with God, the soul is somehow God through participation. Although it is not God as perfectly as it will be in the next life, it is like the shadow of God. Being the shadow of God through this substantial transformation, it performs in this measure in God and through God what God does in the soul.

A reciprocal love is thus formed between God and the soul, like the marriage union and surrender, in which the goods of both are possessed by both together. The soul loves God through God, loves God in God and loves God on account of who God is.

The soul enjoys God by means of God, delights in God alone, without any creatures, enjoys God on account of who God is. The soul praises God and is grateful to God for the natural and spiritual goods it has received, delights in praising God and is grateful because of what God is.

The soul is awakened in God in gentleness and love and experiences the breathing of God within it. The soul knows "all things in God are life" (Jn 1:3-4) and "In God all things live and are and move." (Acts 17:28) In this awakening all things disclose the beauties of their being, power, loveliness, and graces and the root of their duration and life. For the soul is conscious of how all creatures, earthly and heavenly, have their life, direction, and strength in God.

The Awakening

Here lies the remarkable delight of this awakening: the soul knows creatures through God and not God through creatures.

There are no words to describe the love that flows from this awakening. It is a spiration which God produces in the soul, in which, by that awakening of the knowledge of the Godhead, God breathes the Holy Spirit into the soul, rousing its love with divine excellence according to what it beholds in God.

Awaken and enlighten us, Lord, that we might know and love the blessings which You ever propose to us, and that we might understand that You have moved to bestow favors on us and have remembered us.

Publisher's Note

Bear & Company is publishing this series of creation-centered mystic/prophets to bring to the attention and prayer of peoples today the power and energy of the holistic mystics of the Western tradition. One reason Western culture succumbs to boredom and to violence is that we are not being challenged by our religious traditions to be all we can be. This is also the reason that many sincere spiritual seekers go East for their mysticism — because the West is itself out of touch with its deepest spiritual guides. The format Bear & Company has chosen in which to present these holistic mystic/prophets is deliberate: We do not feel that more academically styled books on our mystics are what everyday believers need. Rather, we wish to get the mystics of personal and social transformation off our dusty shelves and into the hearts and minds and bodies of our people. To do this we choose a format that is ideal for meditation, for imaging, for sharing in groups and in prayer occasions. We rely on primary sources for the texts but we let the author's words and images flow from her or his inner structure to our deep inner selves.

BOOKS OF RELATED INTEREST
BY BEAR & COMPANY

MEDITATIONS WITH
HILDEGARD OF BINGEN
by Gabriele Uhlein

MEDITATIONS WITH
JULIAN OF NORWICH
by Brendan Doyle

MEDITATIONS WITH
MECHTILD OF MAGDEBURG
by Sue Woodruff

MEDITATIONS WITH
MEISTER ECKHART
by Matthew Fox

MEDITATIONS WITH
TEILHARD DE CHARDIN
by Blanche Gallagher

MEDITATIONS WITH
TERESA OF AVILA
by Camille Campbell

ORIGINAL BLESSING
A Primer in Creation Spirituality
by Matthew Fox

Contact your local bookseller or write:
BEAR & COMPANY
P.O. Drawer 2860
Santa Fe, NM 87504